WHO IS HE?

RAY LAUBS

Who is He?

ISBN 978-1-64945-996-1

Printed in the United States of America

Copyright @ 2020 Ray Laubs

For Speaking engagements by Ray Laubs send an email to: lizardmen101@gmail.com
I will personally respond to your request.

Scripture references were taken from the King James version of the bible, biblegateway.com public domain.

Preface

I'm writing this book as fast as I can. It is a compilation of short stories. Some of the stories, will not be in chronological sequence, however most are. This is absolutely not all inclusive concerning the things I've seen and have experienced. There are many things left unsaid. There are no hyperboles (fancy word for exaggerations) in this book, the accounts are true and as accurate as I remember them. The spirit of God has laid it on my heart to get to writing it, in fact He has been dealing with me over the last 10 years to write it and is now, "on my case" to get it done. I was originally going to title the book "Who am I?", as in who am I that God would use, but considered the book is for His glory, not mine. The title "Who is He?" is directed at God, hence the capital H. The sole purpose is for you the reader to draw closer and be used of the Lord.

> There is a great sense of urgency to get this published, so without any further ado....

Contents

The beginning of it	6
Taking a switch	7
Happy Trails	7
A child's prayer	8
Dreamscape	8
The good news	9
Keith Green	10
Conviction in Japan	10
Angels on the melt deck	11
Conversion	12
Lights out	15
Spiritual warfare	16
White spots	18
Outside looking in	19
Miracles 1 Cor 12	21
Old folks	23
Water when fasting	24
Chicken, not dinner	25
Opening/closing doors	25
Chicken is served	27
The piano lady	28
Church in the vale	29
Royal Rangers	31
The marble shop	34
Tiny	37

From the other side	39
Locked box	40
Witnessing	40
God's Great Mercy	41
The chapter of failure	42
Lucky Charms	43
Hole in one	44
Grandma knows best	45
Oak Forest	45
Other religions	47
1 Cor 13	48
Broken Toe	49
Out of the coma	50
Heaven	51

The beginning of it

My journey began in October of 1965. There was a dividing line between life and death. The delivery was a most difficult one and my mother was given a choice, her life or that of the child. She unselfishly said: "Let the baby live". We both survived. This was a moment in time where it took the intervention of God for me to be here and the start of this pilgrimage. You see, God has a plan for my life.

Every Sunday was a battlefield for as long as I could remember. Mom would have 5 kids to get dressed and get ready for Sunday school and church. Dad wouldn't be much of a help and would often be working on a night shift the previous night. One memorable Sunday morning, mom had been stressed to the breaking point. She had asked dad if he was going to go to church with us and he said no. She walked out of the living room and into the kitchen, and all you hear next is: *glug, glug, glug, glug* as she is pouring a couple gallons of his homemade wine down the drain in the sink. He gets up and looks out in the kitchen and, with fire in *her* voice, she yells back at him, "If you're not going to church with us, then you're not going to be sitting here drinking this slop"! He never said a word but instead, went back to the living room and sat down.

Taking a switch

When I was somewhere around 8 years old maybe as old as 10? (That's a tough age for any boy) we had a dog and his name was Hanns. I was having a rough day and was really frustrated. I went out with a switch, not quite sure but it was probably lilac, and took my frustration out on the dog by swatting him a couple times. He didn't deserve that. There was an angel that appeared to me and convicted me. That made me cry. I felt really bad for the dog but the damage had already been done. He wasn't bleeding or anything, but still, I had hurt him for no other reason but for my own selfishness.

Happy Trails

Further into our school years we made friends with the neighbor kids. We were somewhere around 8-9-10 years old and quite adventurous. The woods behind our house was laced with trails to each of our homes as us wild little Indians would beat the vegetation back with our feet making many trips during the week. There was a dump site in the woods that we would all frequently visit. We had discovered a plethora of cool things such as metal Tonka trucks and dozers. One time I found a set of Craig power play car speakers mounted inside a hard-shell case. One of the kids found a bible with a green binding and being the renegades we were, one of the gang said something about bibles wouldn't burn. Out came the matches. This book was a little on the wet side and you guessed it, it didn't burn.

A Childs prayer
My one older sister would have us say our prayers before bed time. I remember trying to be funny and asked God to protect us from the bobcats. He did and to this day I have never been attacked, Praise God!

Dreamscape
Every now and then I had a reoccurring dream from as far back as I could remember. It went something like this:
There was a can of charcoal lighter fluid in the middle of the basement floor. I was in "army" clothes and if it were possible, I was laying under the freezer. These little devils were jumping out of the image on the side of the can and I was doing battle against them.
I would immediately wake up. I had that same exact dream many times over the years and would never fully understand it until I had a true spiritual encounter with God on 24 December 1990. The meaning was a revelation into the spiritual warfare that I would be encountering.

The Good News

There was a man who came through our neighborhood one summer looking for kids to have a bible retreat. He ran into our clan and most of us went to hear what he had to say.

There was a lady who lived down the road about a quarter of a mile and she allowed him to set up on her front porch and have bible school for us kids. That was really cool of her to do that.

It was a shaded porch and the concrete was cool when you sat on it, but we didn't mind sitting on the ground. (and besides, who would really want a half dozen, sweaty, smelly neighborhood kids sitting on your good furniture?) One really hot day she brought us out some cold drinks, bless her heart.

I don't remember the man's name, but the most important thing is this: Some sow, some water, but it is God who gives the increase, and again the scripture says; My word will not return unto me void, but it will accomplish the thing where I sent it.

One of the kids in our rag tag band has become a preacher. I have my own paper on the wall, but what is that without God? Christ said I am the vine you are the branch and except you abide in me and I in you, you can do nothing.

The man had given us some blocks, Gold, black, red and white. There were some verses on them, but I don't recall what they were. I have prayed for that man over the years, thanking God for his efforts and his work. He will have his reward in heaven I'm sure. What are you doing for God to advance His kingdom? Do you really need to be led to do something for Jesus and why haven't you just taken the initiative?

Keith Green concert
  Sometime back in the real late 70's, my brother, sister and I were part of a youth group. The leaders took our group to see Keith Green at Messiah College. I could tell there were ministering angels all over that place, coming and going with great excitement!
  In retrospect, man, that guy could play the piano!

Conviction in Japan.
  I was in the USMC between November 83 and November 87. I was with the squadron VMFA-333 out of Beaufort SC. They are no longer in business as they were disbanded back near the beginning of the gulf crisis in 1990. During my time with them we had traveled on a couple WestPac tours hitting Japan, Korea and the Philippines.
  One night in Japan during one my many nights out on the town, the spirit of God was dealing

with me with such great conviction. I had no idea what to do or where to go. It was not a happy place I can assure you. I quickly rustled up a number for the chaplain's office and called him. It was late into the night and I woke him from his sleep. We had agreed to meet the following morning. I was still troubled by God's conviction, but I knew in my heart while talking with this guy, he didn't have what I needed, something was lacking. Time passed and I continued on doing what I had been doing with still no real commitment to Jesus.

Angels on the melt deck

I was working in a foundry prior to my surrender to Christ. There was a Christian man working on one of the automatic molding machines. "Something" told me to go back and talk with him. He was talking to me about Jesus and I really don't remember what all he had said. The one thing that has always stuck with me as I was walking away, was saying to myself "I don't know what it is he has, but that is what I need"!

I was having another one of those days where it seemed as if everything was stacked against me. I don't remember what all it was that happened that day. I was choked up and chatting with God and said to Him that I couldn't take anymore and if one more thing came against me, then I was going to walk out of there. I was walking across the melt deck behind the huge cast iron furnaces and God opened my spiritual eyes. I saw on my left, to my right and out in front of me, 3 angels with swords and shields. I immediately had a new strength knowing I was being protected and there was no way, anyone or anything could rise up against those angels that God had put in place! Keep in mind that I hadn't completely surrendered to Jesus yet and I was still closing the bars down about every night, after all, that's what Marines do, right? But God commendeth his love toward us, in that, while we were yet sinners, Christ died for us.

Conversion
December 1990, I had been shutting the bars down after work. I worked in a town probably 20 miles from home and delighted myself in spending my hard-earned money in the local establishments, I'm sure they appreciated that also. Quite often and with more and more frequency, I found my conversations with the other patrons drifting toward the things of God, maybe not all night but nonetheless, still the topic of God was brought up frequently.
Near Christmas time I was heading home in the wee hours of the morning, passing out at the wheel after shutting down the local watering

hole. Something grabbed me and threw me up against the driver's door and yelled at me "What do you think you're doing boy, you better get with it"! There was no one else in the truck. Then it happened again a few nights later. After that, I got alone with God and said "Okay God, you have my attention".

December 24, 1990 I was sitting in my room thinking about Christmas and how we are to be celebrating the birth of Christ and just how materialistic it all has become. I said to the Lord, "Help me do what I have to before I back out", and just that fast I was up getting the wheel barrow from the carport. Everything in my life that I didn't feel was pleasing to God got tossed in that wheel barrow. I didn't take time to ask anyone, no one told me to do anything, this was personal. I was cleaning my closet out for God.

… It's not that any man should teach you, but the Spirit of God will lead you and guide you into all truth.

The things that got burned that day: over 200 cassettes, a stack of 33 records of rock and roll, pornography, gambling related items and who knows what all. I did not take the time to sort through any of it. All that stuff had one thing in common, it all burned the same.

I was standing beside the fire and said to the Lord, "Here I am", and I meant it. That was the one defining moment in my entire life. It was at that very moment that He gave me a peace that I had never experienced before.

The closest church to the house at that time was probably 2 miles away, it was a Pentecostal church.

I didn't know anything about religions or creeds or anything really. I was good and ignorant.

In January of 1991, we were in the Sunday evening service when it dawned on me that I hadn't eaten anything all day. (Can someone say – fasting?) My heart and mind were consumed with seeking Christ and the previous thought quickly faded as I once again, started seeking Him with all my heart. Near the end of the service, folks started drifting toward the alter and I joined them. Some people were hollering, the visiting preacher went running back the aisle yelling, and someone else was speaking in tongues. The preacher who was over the church was hollering "Praise the Lord, well, praise the Lord"! I had no idea what to say, but as I leaned on the alter and in great ignorance, I said to God, "I'm not here to flop around like a fish out of water like some of these people, I'm here for you". The preacher walked by me and laid his hand on my back. What felt like 500,000 volts of pure supernatural spiritual power boiled from the depths of my soul outward, I knew where the power came from- how the blind could see, the deaf could hear, how the lame were made to walk, and the dead could be raised again!

I had just met the fullness of the Holy Ghost!
…But ye shall receive power, after that the Holy Ghost is come upon you: and ye shall be witnesses unto me both in Jerusalem, and in all Judaea, and in Samaria, and unto the uttermost part of the earth.

<u>Lights out</u>
 Being new to the faith and spiritual experiences, I literally could not get enough of God. I was exhausting myself for more and more of Him and his fullness. The church doors opened at 9am Sunday, I was there at 8am waiting. There was a fire in my soul for Jesus like you wouldn't believe. One night as I was in the church, the end of the service came and went while I was still standing at the alter seeking God. It must have gotten too late for everyone because I was the last man standing. Even the preacher was walking out and someone finally turned the lights out on me, thus ending my time at the alter that night. That sort of hurt my feelings until I learned that not everybody has your vision, neither do they have your level of faith or your stamina.
…And he withdrew himself into the wilderness, and prayed.

Spiritual warfare

I'll never forget my first encounter with a spiritual force. I was young in age. Mom and dad were in the living room watching TV and I was in the kitchen getting a bowl of fruit cocktail. It was late in the evening and probably on the weekend as I was still awake. The basement stairs were right around the corner from where I was standing. All the lights were out except for the dim light beaming from the pole light and the aura from the television radiating from the living room. Combined, they were barely enough for me to see by. Something came running up the wooden stairs and got much louder the closer it got to where I was standing. I took off like a rocket ship into the living room. The sound in the stairwell was loud enough it woke my brother from his slumber. He came running with a flash light while dad grabbed the shotgun. We searched (notice I said we, however I was in the back of the pack) the entire basement and nothing was there. Nothing was knocked off the shelves, all the windows and doors were closed and locked and there was no one down there.

Fast forward a few years after my salvation experience. My dad was into leather work and he truly was a very skilled craftsman. He would gather patterns, photos, templates and just about anything he could make a leather pattern from. He wasn't just into making wallets, though he did make some that have lasted for many years. He would carve and tool raised pictures such as a mountain lion on a log with a pine tree in the back ground. He made a photo album with a raised horse head on the front and a plethora of other items.

He passed away in May of 1984 just shortly after I arrived in Meridian Mississippi for additional training in the Marine Corps. His leather tools and everything sat in the basement up until, I'm guessing- 1994? The Lord led me to fast one day and I found myself in his shop boxing everything up. I went from the one side all the way around to the other.

There was a huge stack of magazines in the corner but I had grown tired and figured, ah, I'll finish it another day. I started walking out of the leather shop but the spirit of God turned me around and marched me right back to that corner.

I flipped through the rags one at a time. Modern railroad today, fur fish and game, sports illustrated,
another railroad rag, and so this went on until I got about half way down through the stack when I pick up a board with the alphabet on it. It was quite a decorative piece and I also noticed it had a couple words on it, yes, no, Ouija …. Hold on Jethro! This just got real!

I started praying in the spirit and took that thing outside to the garden and burned it right then

and there. It was at this point; I got the all clear from God that He had accomplished what needed to be done. Another incident took place at the homestead. I was in the basement scrubbing the grease off of a set of 400 small block Chevrolet engine heads. I was singing songs to God making them up as I went along. It was in February I think, maybe in 1991? Hard to tell, I didn't write this stuff down until now.
Regardless, there was a fire in the woodstove. We had 2 fifty-five gallon drums, one on top of each other and I recall the fire was going good. There was a spirit that picked me up and threw me physically back toward the wood stove a good 8' airborne. God Himself, or an angel He sent, caught me and gently put me back on my feet so that not one hair on my head was out of sorts. I asked the Lord; do I praise you or curse the devil? Craziest thing I ever dealt with. This episode landed me in a lot of arguments with the religious elite.

White spots
A friend of mine had asked me to pray for him because he had white spots on his tongue from chewing tobacco for years. I did and God removed them. White spots are indicative of cancer, especially for those who use tobacco for years on end.

Outside looking in

The atmosphere in the house was really never quite right. After I got out of the Marines I had stayed with my mom for a bit and when I got saved, things really got weird there at the homestead. I would be sleeping and the blankets would be ripped off of me and thrown into the middle of the room. One night I heard a lot of creaking and groaning in the house and figured it was cold outside and warm inside. That is, until an evil force rested on my chest and shoved me 6 inches down in the mattress.

I had been working 10-hour days, six days a week and only getting about two or three hours of sleep with all the spiritual wars going on around me. I was mentally, physically and spiritually exhausted. People at church would offer me advice such as: be careful these things are real, pray over the house, sleep with a bible on your head, sleep with a bible under your pillow, sleep with one on your chest, anoint the house with water, anoint it with oil, quote this verse, quote that verse, and finally someone told me to "Plead the blood of Jesus". (To this day no one has ever been able to tell me what that meant, in fact I challenge you to look it up in your bible, oh that's right, that phrase isn't in there.) So, I did all these things and still the war raged on. I finally gave up and said as much to the Lord, "I quit, good night" and meant it. I went to sleep and sometime in the night His spirit shot through me like a bolt of lightning and He wasn't happy with that decision. At that very moment, He gave me peace and stopped the wars. He allowed me to go through all that to show me, if you want anything, victory, deliverance, peace, anything at all, it will come from Him and Him alone. It will not come because you know some bible verses or do some religious acts. He is the one that is in control.

I still went through some torments. I heard popping in the room one night and I laid there and told the Lord I was just going to sing songs until he sent his spirit to clean this mess up. I sang songs to him, made them up as I went along for the most part, long
into the night and then all of a sudden, it sounded like a fire in a popcorn factory. *Pop, creak, pop, pop, creak, pop* and the air itself grew lighter and I could feel the presence of evil leaving the room. I heard one loud creaking in the hallway and that is when I got scared, real scared and I surrendered my entire being to Christ and I said to Him, "Lord, I don't know what is going on around here, but I'm trusting you with all my heart, mind, soul and body.", and immediately I was up in the middle of the air above my bed. I looked down across the bridge of my nose, but there was no nose to see. I tried closing my eyelids as tight as I could, but

there were no eyelids to close. I was out of this physical body. The Holy Ghost carried me immediately into His presence. I did not see the kingdom of heaven at this time; I was only in His presence. I will make an attempt to explain what it was like, however, there are no words in our language that can remotely come close to it: Extreme Peace, Extreme Love, Extreme Happiness, Extreme Liberty, Extreme Joy, Extreme Exuberance, Extreme Freedom, Extreme... and my words fail.

I remember dancing violently in His presence for a time. He didn't say anything, although I knew He was going to put me back into this body and I begged him not to, I didn't want to come back. "Just a little longer, just a little longer", I remember pleading with Him.

But you see the end of this part, here I am telling the stories that God has given me.

Miracles:
1 Corinthians 12 King James Version (KJV)
12 Now concerning spiritual gifts, brethren, I would not have you ignorant.

2 Ye know that ye were Gentiles, carried away unto these dumb idols, even as ye were led.

3 Wherefore I give you to understand, that no man speaking by the Spirit of God calleth Jesus accursed: and that no man can say that Jesus is the Lord, but by the Holy Ghost.

⁴ Now there are diversities of gifts, but the same Spirit.

⁵ And there are differences of administrations, but the same Lord.

⁶ And there are diversities of operations, but it is the same God which worketh all in all.

⁷ But the manifestation of the Spirit is given to every man to profit withal.

⁸ For to one is given by the Spirit the word of wisdom; to another the word of knowledge by the same Spirit;

⁹ To another faith by the same Spirit; to another the gifts of healing by the same Spirit;

¹⁰ To another the working of miracles; to another prophecy; to another discerning of spirits; to another divers kinds of tongues; to another the interpretation of tongues:

¹¹ But all these worketh that one and the selfsame Spirit, dividing to every man severally as he will.

Old folks
 Right after I got saved, I was still working at the same job. Many people saw what God had done in my life, turning me from a drunk to a saint overnight and many of my friends were completely perplexed by this transformation.
 One Thanksgiving Day as I was heading past my place of employment to go to my brother's house, it dawned on me that I had several pies in the car and there were security guards working. I pulled up to the guard shack and gave them a pecan pie. I told the guard that I was thinking of them as they had to work while the rest of us were with our families and handed him the pie. It made him cry.
 When the weekend was over and we all headed back to the grind, everyone in the facility knew what I had done. There were some who openly let me know they appreciated that deed.
 ... That thine alms may be in secret: and thy Father which seeth in secret himself shall reward thee openly.
 One of the guards I befriended had invited me up to his place and so I went. His family lived high up on the mountain and it was like a step back into time. I thought this was pretty cool, dirt road and all. His mother was a God-fearing woman and raised her children with the knowledge of God. Sister Welsh I will call her.

Every time we got together; well you know where those conversations went!

We ended up having Saturday night services in her living room and the spirit of God moved in that old house let me tell you!

I hung around this older generation for a bit and often times I would hear them make references to what God used to do or what they used to see God do and one day I got alone with the Lord and told Him, "I'm tired of hearing what you used to do, here I am, use me", and He did.

…Verily, verily, I say unto you, He that believeth on me, the works that I do shall he do also; and greater works than these shall he do; because I go unto my Father.

Water when fasting

Early on in my Christian walk I was doing some uneducated and dangerous fasting. I wasn't drinking water or eating for a number of days, in retrospect, I'm certain God wasn't in it. Nonetheless, one day as I went to lay down, I had zero strength, zero energy, and as I went to lay on the bed I said as much to the Lord, even something in the lines if He didn't intervene, I wasn't going to make it. I was sleeping soundly when an angel was sent from God with a pitcher of water. The angel showed up and gave me a drink. Immediately I had great strength and great energy. It was like no water I had ever drank before. God intervened in my reckless behavior or else I probably wouldn't have survived that one. I didn't do that again.

Chicken, not dinner

I was sitting at the table with the mountain people mentioned earlier, having a time of prayer. I'm not sure how long we were there. My friend's rooster was trying to crow but couldn't, it was all scratchy sounding and raspy. Mid stride of a prayer request, I said to the Lord, "and while you're at it, will you fix that chicken?" and He did. Moments later that bird crowed very loud and clear and it was indeed the first time since my friend had owned him that it ever crowed like that… Casting all your care upon him; for he careth for you.

Opening and closing doors

Early in my Christian walk, I believed that God was going to send me to Africa.

I was working in a metal fabrication shop and a customer came in wanting a bunch of odd shaped metal plates cut. I inquired as to their purpose and he explained he was going to use them to make cinder block molds for a missionary trip to Africa.

The locals were going to make their own blocks with it and build their own church.

I asked him how one goes about getting on the list to go over there. He said that he operates the show and the list was full. However, every time on these trips, someone always backs out. I told him to put my name on the backup roster. I was in the number one slot as no one else had signed up yet as a backup.

Red lights, Bells, Whistles – they were all going off inside my head and I was overwhelmed! This was it! I knew I was to go over there and this door just opened wide!

As time passed, I kept in communication with the man, checking in on a weekly basis. We were getting down to the wire for the departure and he said he couldn't believe it. No one had backed out. It was the first time ever in all the years he organized this mission trip that no one has backed out... These things saith He that is holy, He that is true, He that hath the key of David, He that openeth and no man shutteth, and shutteth and no man openeth.

God closed that door.

Be careful of your divine imaginations. Not every thought, not every dream is of God. Pray for discernment and stay humble.

Chicken is served

A very good friend of mine was really, well, old enough to be my grandmother. Many times, we would watch early VHS videos of James Robinson, Charles Stanley or some of the other gospel preachers. She was indeed the grandmother I never had. Every Sunday after church she would invite me over for a chicken dinner. She never got out much and didn't have a lot of visitors, so this always made her week. I'd pop in, she would yell the doors open. It was a very beautiful time.

She shared with me that her daughter had breast cancer. The mammogram was positive, the biopsy came back positive and the doctor had scheduled her for a radical mastectomy.

  Shortly after on a Sunday as I popped in the door, I saw her daughter sitting at the table. I approached her in a soft voice and asked her if I could pray for her. She started crying and said please do. I laid my hand on her shoulder and with true agape love and absolute compassion, I prayed this prayer: "Lord, in Jesus name, will you heal Shirley of this cancer? For your glory God, for your glory, amen."

  Shirley went back to the doctor and asked him to reexamine her before he touched her. He did and there was nothing there to be found.

Jesus had compassion on them. ...

  There came a time when I had been fasting and praying when God told me to separate myself from my friend. I shared this with her and explained that it was neither good nor bad but it is what God had said to me. She said she felt God in what I was saying and so we parted ways. I was troubled by that. Not long after, she passed away and even as I type this, it saddens my heart. She was my friend.

<u>The piano lady</u>
There was another friend of mine who was exceptionally gifted at playing the piano. I called her one night to see how she was doing. She had a migraine headache and even whispering over the phone reverberated inside her head making her cry even more. I asked her if I could pray with her and she agreed to it. With a quiet voice, I began: "Father, in the name of Jesus…" and that's all I got out. She started laughing hysterically on the other end of the phone shouting: "You are not going to believe this!" and I replied, "Oh yes I will"! She went onto say, "As you started to pray, that migraine went straight out through the top of my head!"… And whatsoever ye shall ask in my name, that will I do, that the Father may be glorified in the Son.

Church in the vale
 There was a small church over the mountain and up the valley, who knows, 30-40 miles out? The owner had a construction business and was a hardworking man. He was scratching around one day and prayed about fixing it up and holding services there and that pleased God!
 He did a great job refurbishing the old place. Fresh oak, tongue and groove across the ceiling all sealed up with a semi-gloss clear coat varnish. The place was really neat and warm.
 We ended up holding services over there for who knows how long.
One day as I stepped in the door of the church, God spoke to me and said, "I want you to go up there and pray for that woman". So, I went up where "that" woman was sitting and I gave her a once over, looking for what might be wrong.
She had a cast on her lower leg/foot. I asked her what happened and she said she broke her ankle. Then I asked her if she believed that God could heal her and she said yes. Just then the spirit of God told me to tell her to get up and I did.
 The preacher perceived that God was doing something and came over and started praying, but it was too late. God had already healed her ankle the moment she stood up. She never even had as much as an itch in that ankle from that moment on.
 Same church as before, only this time there was a preacher from Alabama that came through

town. He was given the reigns of the church. His mother was visiting and she fell inside during one of the services and hurt her knee.

She sought medical attention but nothing would correct her ailment, and finally after many trips to doctor's office etcetera, the insurance company finally said no more. Bottom line: there was no more money from the insurance company.

A little bit of time had passed and I encountered her and a few other ministers at a home. She was sitting in a recliner with her feet up in the air. We were talking about miracles and the spirit of God told me to tell her to get up. I did and that thing went "POP"!

It was quite loud and I was thinking to myself as I cringed, did I do the right thing here God? She stood there for a couple seconds and I asked her "how does your knee feel now?" and she replied "Better!"

… And a woman having an issue of blood twelve years, which had spent all her living upon physicians, neither could be healed of any, came behind *him*, and touched the border of his garment: and immediately her issue of blood stanched.

Royal Rangers

I was a part of a denomination one time called the Pentecostal Holiness. With the preachers consent I chiseled out a ministry known as the Royal Rangers. The church was really a small one and we didn't have any kids that attended there but what the heck, how hard can that be right?

It got off the ground with as many as 5 boys I think and God started to move.

We were camping at Caledonia state park in south central Pennsylvania. The agenda for that night was to walk down to the nature center and watch a movie about birds of prey. There was a bit of a hic up in this plan as it was raining pretty hard and we really didn't want to get soaked. The one young man had asked me if I would pray and ask God to make it quit raining. I told him no. I said, "Mike, you do it." This young fellow in a sincere prayer asked the Lord to hold the rain off until we got down there and got back. You see, God wants kids to know He hears them!

The group of us stepped out onto the road and one of the boys chirped up with "Hey! It quit raining"!

We hiked down through the dark forest and watched the movie. I learned a little bit about Peregrine falcons, that they make a ball with their feet as they strike and don't just grab with their claws.

The hike back was just as dark and as soon as we set foot inside the camp, you guessed it, just as Mike had prayed, it opened up and P-O-U-R-E-D!

... Ask, and it shall be given you; seek, and ye shall find; knock, and it shall be opened unto you: For every one that asketh receiveth; and he that seeketh findeth; and to him that knocketh it shall be opened.

A friend of mine was attending an Assembly of God church and had a Royal Ranger ministry going with them. We decided to get both our groups together and have a camp out in the mountains above James Buchanan's birth place. This secluded spot lays between Mercersburg and McConnellsburg here in south central Pennsylvania on route 16. If you bat your eye, you'll shoot past the entrance. We had put a lot of planning into this event and wanted the boys to remember it, *this was our plan.

Kevin and I had made several trips up there, we cleared the campsite of the underbrush and rocks, the trail between the campsite and where we were going to build the fire had to be blazed, and getting the ceremony fire set up.

Then came the weekend of the campout. One of his boys that was there, had a brand-new pair of wire frame glasses. Like any kid, he was running all over the side of that mountain.

I was in the camp and here he came sobbing, saying that he lost his glasses.

There was a creek that was completely lined with sand stone rocks and boulders that flowed down through the area. It might have been as narrow as 8' and perhaps as wide as 20' in places. I asked him if he lost them on this side of the creek or the other side and all I got back was a stuffy nosed kid answer, "I don't know".

I start grumbling to God, "Great, now I'm going to have to reimburse his dad, what am I supposed to do"?

I was walking up through the woods and God gave me a vision. He showed me the glasses falling into the water and the current pushing them under a rock.

I thanked the Lord for the vision and went on to remind Him that there were 4 million rocks in that creek. Then a cloud of peace settled down over me and I gave no thought to what I was doing. I went over to the bank and grabbed a stick. Again, without giving thought, I hopped onto the rocks out into the middle of the creek. From where I was standing, the sun was reflecting off the surface of the water blinding me from seeing anything. With the same thoughtless approach, in one motion, I jabbed that stick under a rock at my feet and lifted it up. Those glasses were hanging on the end of that stick.

... go thou to the sea, and cast a hook, and take up the fish that first cometh up; and when thou hast opened his mouth, thou shalt find a piece of money: that take, and give unto them for me and thee.

The marble shop

I started collecting marbles because of my wife. She found a sulphide at an estate sale. It was approximately 2" in diameter, clear glass with a small ceramic dog "floating" inside of it. I was captivated by that. I said to her about collecting those types of marbles and she was cool with it, that is until we went to the antique shop and saw the price they were fetching. It was at this point I said, "Why don't we make our own, how hard can that be?" and so this part of the journey began. I could go on all day about this adventure but I have already written a book on it called "The Making of Sulphides".

While in the glass shop one day, the Lord put a date in my head. I hurriedly grabbed a black marker and wrote the date on the plywood wall. I knew it had significance but had no idea what it was about. When that day finally came (I'm thinking it was a year and a half notice) it was the discovery that the stained-glass sheets I had were compatible with my clear. This opened up a whole new venue in the marble shop.

There was talk in the marble community about what was the most vanes anyone had seen in a catseye marble. Someone said 9 was the most they had seen, and of course, me being the eccentric person I am, thought why not 12 vanes!

I prayed about it. I knew what I wanted to do but had no clue how to get to achieve it. I had asked God to show me the way, then not long after that when I was in the shop, the thoughts came to me, very quickly and in rapid succession:

Take the circumference of 360 degrees, divide that by the number of vanes, saw metal shims at 30 degrees, stand up pieces of your color in the kiln and put the shims between them, blow a ball on the end of the pipe, open the end of it up and flatten it out so there is a round disk with a hole in the center. Pre heat that and pick up the pieces of glass, submerge all that in the crucible gathering clear glass up over the entire thing. Draw a vacuum on the pipe. Stretch it out and viola - there you have it. Those marbles sold like hot cakes. The glass shop has been shut down for a couple years now since being on night shift and I still have people requesting those 12 vane catseye marbles.

During the years I was operating the marble shop, God had used me from time to time. We would go to shows all over the place from the far reaches of West Virginia to Marlboro

Massachusetts to Ohio and all points in between, not to mention the many contacts all over the world.

I have been blessed to have had the opportunity to witness to many people and share Gods love, mercy, and forgiveness. I have talked with people who were bi sexual, Satanist, strung out on heroin and all walks of life.

We were at a show in Columbus Ohio and the Lord told me to go over and talk with this one big fellow, so I did. I asked him if he knew Jesus and he said he did. I explained why I was asking and he was good with that. When that show was over, he was returning home with his wife on his motorcycle. They were involved in an accident and he died.

A great friend of mine had a website set up for marbles, MarbleAlan is what he went by. He was from Jacksonville Florida and made a living by buying and selling marbles. He was an educated man and had at one point been a forensic anthropologist.

One night in the chat room off to the side of his web page, the topic came up on what one needed to do to be saved. The religious elite were fighting openly and it was truly a disgusting mess. Alan asked me to join him in a side chat room away from the noise. A lesbian friend of ours joined us in that room. Alan asked me, "Ray, what is the truth"? So, I told him. No one is good enough to get to heaven. I'm not, the preachers aren't, absolutely no one. God saw that and sent his son Jesus into this world to fix this mess. They killed him and on the third day, he was raised again from the dead. All you have to do, is ask Him to forgive you for all you've done wrong and go on to live for Him." He thanked me and not much longer after that he passed away from multi organ stage 4 cancer.

   …Preach the word; be instant in season, out of season;

Tiny

 There were a few years where I had been working in my glass shop making marbles and paperweights on the side. A lot of what I made I was selling on eBay. It was a profitable venture as I was always pushing the envelope with new ideas, making designs that other glass artist were not doing. I even published a book on the work I was doing in the glass shop.
 Tiny had purchased a lot of marbles off of me and one night through eBay he had asked me if I would be interested in taking a special order. We exchanged phone numbers and it might have been 10 o'clock at night when he called me. He described what he was looking for, 1" marbles with a black rectangle inside with red letters GRMC on the rectangle, probably 100 of them. I told him I would give it some thought on how I

would approach the project and throw some numbers at him. He asked me if I knew what GRMC meant and I told him no. He said it stood for Grim Reapers Motorcycle Club.

I got alone with Jesus and asked Him, is this something I want to get involved in? The spirit of God replied to me, "Hear him out".

It might have been the following night when we were back on the phone talking. Up until this point I hadn't heard Tiny use any curse words. I asked him if he knew Jesus and to my surprise, he said he did. Herein lies the religious mind-blowing event that knocked my hat off. After all, every Christian is told by some man/woman that God wouldn't have you in a place like that.

He said he wouldn't allow his brothers to use the Lord's name in vain around him but at the same time, he wouldn't meddle into their personal affairs either. Tiny was the treasurer of their local chapter. Through several other conversations, he shared stories with me on how he had led several of his brothers to Jesus and shortly thereafter they had been killed in a gun fight. God is a spirit, He is the only true and living God, there is no other. He is not a religion. He desires everyone to come to Him. He will use who-so-ever is willing, where-so-ever you are, and He will use you if you are willing to humble yourself. Lay aside the teachings of men and venture out in obedience and see where God takes you. This whole thing with God is a relationship, based solely on the work that Christ has done. Are you willing to go out on a limb where you are and just obey?

From the other side

I was walking through the living room one day and I heard my brother's wife yell at me from the spiritual realm. She screamed "Ray, save me!". I turned around and yelled right back into the room: "I can't do that, only Jesus can!" I thought okay, that was weird. A couple days later I found out, that was the very moment she died.

My brother John wasn't in the best of health, in fact he ended up in the hospital. He had beaten cancer once before but this time it was different. He was plagued with other ailments. Diabetes had already taken his vision, and his leg, now it was round 2 of prostate cancer.

I was at work and it was near 8 in the morning. I heard him saying from the spiritual realm, "It's not as bad as you think". Ten minutes later his son calls my cell phone and tells me that John had just passed away.

Locked box

The church had an issue with the dusk to dawn lights that surrounded the parking lot. I know about electricity and was trying to figure out why they weren't working. The preacher and I went through all the panel boxes and all the breakers were still in the on position. I found a lone panel box outside on the wall and behind the bushes. I thought that perhaps it had something to do with the lights.

We tried every key in the church to open that lock and none of them fit it. We exhausted all means except for bolt cutters. I prayed and asked God, "Will you do one of your miracles?", and without thinking, I reached out, grabbed the lock and yanked down on it and it opened right up.

Witnessing:
There was an older lady, Sister Mary I called her. She loved the Lord with all her heart and though being well up into her years, she held a bible study every Monday night for the kids in the trailer park. I would go up and help her out but really, I think she just enjoyed the company.

One Monday night I was heading up to the study and I saw a man leaning on a railing at the fishery and God told me to go talk to him. I pulled in and as soon as I got out of the truck, I heard a voice in my ear say, "he's going to smash your teeth out".

I recognized the man from back when I was still in school. We chatted a little and I asked him if he ever accepted Jesus and his reply was "I'm not ready". We caught up on idle yap and

somehow, I got to talking about this road I found that led up into the mountains. It became a road trip. Numerous times that evening I tried everything to persuade him to accept Christ as his savior, but I was always met with the same response as before. It was after midnight; I was tired and dropped him off at his apartment. He invited me in for a soda and as we sat at his table, I asked him, "Lewis, do you want to get saved or not?" He said I guess so. I growled at him "Then take your hat off and let's pray". When the prayer was over, he sat there crying, saying he felt clean inside.
 I missed the bible study that night.

God's great mercy
 Many times, I have witnessed to whoever God wanted me to, mostly as surprises from the spirit in random places. A lot of times I have seen where those I had talked with concerning their souls, have passed away within days or weeks of our conversations. I view these situations as God showing His Great mercy in not wanting anyone to go to hell. Please I beg you, obey God.
 For those who are back slid and trying to catch back up, news flash ….. God still loves you and wants you to come home !

The chapter on failure

I can honestly say there are no failures. Most of what one would call a failure really isn't that, they are incidents of disobedience or flat out sin – same difference.

These incidents paralyze you, create regret, cause guilt and in the end renders one immobile and left feeling defeated, then nothing gets done for Him.

How do I know? Because I, ladies and gentlemen, am the number one violator and have disappointed the Lord Himself more than I care to recall.

I will not list my violations as I refuse to live under that bondage. I have regrets but will rise above them and live in His light. His grace is sufficient, His mercy is more than enough. He has completed the redeeming work. Now it is up to you and me to follow in obedience.

Whatever you do, do NOT put your eyes on man. They will fail you, they will upset your applecart, and they will do things that will overturn your faith. Instead you need to look to Him who is invisible. The author and finisher of your faith, the alpha and the omega, the beginning and the end.

The closer you get to God and the deeper you get into spiritual things with Him, you will find yourself standing and working alone. Very few people walk in the deeper places in God. When the Lord directs you, he isn't automatically directing the entire assembly, he isn't necessarily guiding you *and* your spouse. He is leading one person, and that is you. The time to obey is in the moment of His beckoning. Ten minutes later is ten minutes too late. You will stand alone when you obey Him, and the enemy wants nothing more than for you to quit, flounder, or disobey. God will not always come back around for a second chance, especially if it's a miracle in the making. If God has sent you, He will equip you. A lot does not get done because of disobedience, fear and unbelief.

<u>Lucky charms</u>
  It was a hot summer afternoon as I was heading home from work. It really was a blister of a day.
  I was about half way home when I had passed by a man who was walking on the opposite side of the road with a rifle in his hand. Right after I passed him, I looked in the side view mirror of my crew cab pick up truck and noticed, this guy was truly in duress. I could tell by the way he was lifting his feet to walk.
  I turned the truck around and pulled up alongside of him and told him to get in. He put the rifle in the back seat and explained it was only an airsoft, (for your understanding it was an air rifle), but I didn't care either way.
  The water jug I had from work only had a little bit of warm water in the bottom. This really

made me feel bad, in that, it was my opinion that wasn't enough water this man needed. I was further disappointed in that, I had nothing to give him to eat for energy.

He was covered in little wee tattoos, for some strange reason I envisioned it as if someone had sprinkled lucky charms cereal all over him. Please understand when I write this, I'm not making fun of him nor am I judging him. Maybe I should have left this part out of the book, but this is what went through my head at the time.

I shared with him the gospel of Jesus the Christ, (it might sound strange, but Christ means: The anointed one. It's not Jesus' last name). God said to me, "He is mine".

I took him where he wanted to go and dropped him off. I offered to buy him some water bottles and food but he declined. I have never saw him again.

Be not forgetful to entertain strangers: for thereby some have entertained angels unawares.

Hole in one

One day while running a radial arm drill, the Spirit of God was on me. Every motion was as smooth as glass, drilling one hole, into the next, using the calipers to check the tolerances then onto the next part. I discovered the owner of the shop had been watching me and he said "you do good work". As he walked away, that supernatural anointing went with it. It wasn't as smooth without that anointing.

Grandma knows best
I was working in a weld shop one time and God spoke to me to talk with this one boy. The conversation started with: "Do you know anything about Jesus?" He started replying that his grandmother knows all about that. I interrupted him and told him that God had instructed me to talk to him and this was not about his grandma. I shared with him the gospel and told him bluntly that he needed to seek God. The Lord doesn't tell you to talk to someone for no reason. As witnesses, we are His mouth piece for His motives. I said before that often times when I'm instructed to witness to someone, they end up dying. A week or so later, this fellow died in a car wreck. It is so important that you obey God when it comes to sharing the gospel... Neither is there salvation in any other: for there is none other name under heaven given among men, whereby we must be saved.

Oak forest
There were a few of us family members out galivanting one weekend and we stopped at this restaurant called "Oak Forest".

It was owned and operated by a Christian lady who just happened to also be a minister of the gospel.

As I walked in the door, the spirit of God told me to go up and talk to some guy at the counter.

I need to explain something here; when I'm instructed to talk to strangers, it's not easy. There is usually a great fear that comes over me because the enemy doesn't want God's word going forth. I've had the enemy many times tell me things in my ear, such as; "he is going to knock your teeth down your throat", and "they don't want to hear what you have to say" and the list goes on. Here is where you must stand on your faith knowing that you are fulfilling God's plan and God's will. Stay humble and stay obedient my friends.

As most conversations start, I asked him if he knew Jesus and he gave me some smart answer. I told him God told me to come over and talk to him, but okay. I went to my table, sat down, ordered and eventually was eating my lunch.

This guy comes over and sits down on the empty seat at our table and says, "You're telling me, that God told you to talk to me"? I said that's right and you need to seek Him because He isn't playing games. He wouldn't tell me to talk to someone for no reason.

The man got up and left the restaurant and once again, I have never seen him since.

Other religions
I have seen some preachers from mainstream religions get hateful when someone from another religion comes knocking on their door. When I say hateful, I mean, slamming the door and growling hateful. Gee, I really want what they have. That'll make me change my entire religious beliefs just so I can be like them… not.
I really do love when someone comes to my door. I greet them all with the same greeting: "Come in, are you thirsty, are you hungry, here sit in this chair – it's the best one in the house! I have a story to tell you!" Most often when I have finished telling them about Jesus, they usually never come back. My motive is to win them to Christ, not chase them off by being belligerent. Remember earlier in this book I said when I walked away from that one guy saying, "I don't know what it is he has, but that's what I need", this is my prayer to everyone I chat with. That they walk away saying the same thing to themselves. It's not me or about me, it's not about feelings per se', it is about the presence of God.
That the spirit of God will convict them and draw them to Himself, that they might know the true gospel.
I was out knocking on doors once in the town where the church was located. Some guy answered his door and I started giving him my

spiel, he said not today. I replied, "Okay, well you have a great day!"

I turned and walked away. I got about half way out the driveway when he hollers for me to come back. He asked me, "Why did you walk away so fast and not argue with me like other religious people do"? I told him, "God isn't going to make you serve Him if you don't want to, and I will not shove him on anyone who doesn't want to hear." He heard.

1 Corinthians 13 King James Version (KJV)
13 Though I speak with the tongues of men and of angels, and have not charity, I am become as sounding brass, or a tinkling cymbal.

² And though I have the gift of prophecy, and understand all mysteries, and all knowledge; and though I have all faith, so that I could remove mountains, and have not charity, I am nothing.

³ And though I bestow all my goods to feed the poor, and though I give my body to be burned, and have not charity, it profiteth me nothing.

⁴ Charity suffereth long, and is kind; charity envieth not; charity vaunteth not itself, is not puffed up,

⁵ Doth not behave itself unseemly, seeketh not her own, is not easily provoked, thinketh no evil;

⁶ Rejoiceth not in iniquity, but rejoiceth in the truth;

⁷ Beareth all things, believeth all things, hopeth all things, endureth all things.

⁸ Charity never faileth: but whether there be prophecies, they shall fail; whether there be tongues, they shall cease; whether there be knowledge, it shall vanish away.

⁹ For we know in part, and we prophesy in part.

¹⁰ But when that which is perfect is come, then that which is in part shall be done way.

¹¹ When I was a child, I spake as a child, I understood as a child, I thought as a child: but when I became a man, I put away childish things.

¹² For now we see through a glass, darkly; but then face to face: now I know in part; but then shall I know even as also I am known.

¹³ And now abideth faith, hope, charity, these three; but the greatest of these is charity.

Broken toe
 We were in a midweek church service a few years ago. I couldn't even tell you what the preacher was
talking about or what we had going on at the time. It was at the end of the service and most everybody had filtered out, leaving only a few of us talking in the foyer. I saw the pastor's wife limping pretty bad and asked her what happened. She said she broken her toe. I prayed with her and the Spirit of God moved in a powerful way. We began shouting and praising God! Sue started jumping up and down because that toe was healed!

Out of the coma (caution: this is a bit graphic)
 My wife's uncle and I were friends. He had health issues and needed a stent. He was quite a big man, height wise. The stent he required was the largest they make. The surgery seemed to have gone well but 3 days into this, they had to open him back up. The stent had blocked the flow of blood to his lower bowel and without the blood flow, his guts were dying off.
They cut out the bad intestines and gave him a colostomy for the rest of his life. He was put into a chemically induced coma for about 6 months.
 We would go up to Harrisburg and visit him every weekend. One Sunday I was standing

beside his bed and I heard him in the spirit. He said, "Ray I'm scared". I replied back in an audible voice, "You have every right to be afraid Jim." He responded with, "How is it that you can hear me?" I fired back, "Because Jim this is a spiritual matter and not some religious thing. What you need to do is seek Jesus and make peace with him". That was the end of that conversation.

Sometime later when they brought him back out of the coma, his sister was there. She is a Christian woman. Jim wasn't able to speak because of the breathing tube they had just removed, but he was able to do charades of pointing to his heart and then pointing up. Joanne asked him, "Did you give your heart to Jesus?" and Jim shook his head yes.

Heaven

Up until now I hadn't fully seen heaven. I had caught a glimpse of it – up around the bend per se'. It was the morning of May 6, 2020 and I had just finished dumping a load of scrap metal off at the salvage yard. I felt God moving that morning and figured something was going to happen. As I was driving out the road, the Lord said to me, "What do you want from me"? Without thinking I blurted out, to be used of you as I once was. Immediately heaven was opened to me. His light radiating in heaven is a perfect light, everything is a beautiful white and the thing I remember the most, there were no shadows at all. There was wave after wave of rejoicing and excitement and celebration and I don't have the words for it. If I could even remotely describe it, it would sound something like this- a static storm of exuberant praises exalting Him who sits on the throne! Wave after wave of praises and Great rejoicing!

He revealed His presence – Holy and pure beyond anything you can imagine, and at the same time I saw my own heart and the sin that was in me. I was terrified in His presence. He said to me, "Because you have sinned, do not call on me, I will not hear you", and the spiritual realm was immediately closed. I really had a hard time with all this. It brought me very low to the point where I believed there was no hope for me to ever get to heaven, I really felt doomed. Then the enemy tried everything to get me to blame God. It sounded right but yet, I said to God, "even if there is no hope for me, I will not blame you or your son Jesus. My sins are mine and I am guilty." It has taken a couple weeks of reading the scriptures and accepting Gods promises. I have shed some serious tears, repented and now walk in a holy fear of who He is and what is to come. Though I have been forgiven, I am afraid for those who don't know Jesus, I am afraid for those who will not turn from their evil ways, I am afraid for my own self - a holy fear for Him who sits on the throne. Make no mistake, God is holy and will not accept anything less than that from us.

He has said many times over if you turn from your sin and seek His face, He will hear from heaven and forgive your sin. I have been so blessed since this all has happened and desire to do all I can for Him. There are many verses in the bible to back up repentance and asking for forgiveness. There is a plethora of verses where Jesus isn't going to let go of you either and how you are sealed until the day of redemption by that spirit of promise. Some theologians will argue it but I know where I have walked and who it is that pulled me through, His name is Jesus. You have your part and that is to repent and turn away from sin. Don't you know it's the goodness of God that leads you to repent?

It is so important to get into His word and read it. You need to know what the bible says. Even when Jesus was tempted by Satan, he would say, "It is written". Jesus said, heaven and earth will pass away but my words will not pass away. You need to know what the bible says, you need to believe His promises.

My wife had a headache maybe a week after this started. I prayed for her and Jesus healed her of it immediately.

Walk softly, be holy, and don't grieve the spirit of God by clowning around taking His ways lightly.

One last and very important note:
God will not share His glory with any man.
Whatsoever God does through you, give all
glory and praise to Him, always!

www.ingramcontent.com/pod-product-compliance
Lightning Source LLC
LaVergne TN
LVHW041548060526
838200LV00037B/1193